D1616919

DISCARD

# Flying against the Wind

# Flying against the Wind

A Story about Beryl Markham

by Andy Russell Bowen
illustrations by Shelly O. Haas

A Creative Minds Biography

Carolrhoda Books, Inc./Minneapolis

*For Monnie and Marcia, my oldest friends*
*—A. R. B.*

*With special thanks to Toshanna, Jeanette, and Edwin*
*—S. O. H.*

The author wishes to thank Donald Woods, Kenneth Kibagendi Angwenyi, and Charles Kibagendi Orinda for their interest and help.

Text copyright © 1998 by Andy Russell Bowen
Illustrations copyright © 1998 by Shelly O. Haas

Carolrhoda Books, Inc., c/o The Lerner Publishing Group
241 First Avenue North, Minneapolis, MN 55401 U.S.A.
Website address: www.lernerbooks.com

Library of Congress Cataloging-in-Publication Data

Bowen, Andy Russell.
    Flying against the wind : a story about Beryl Markham / by Andy Russell Bowen ; illustrations by Shelly O. Haas.
        p.   cm. — (Carolrhoda creative minds book)
    Includes bibliographical (p.   ) references and index.
    Summary: A biography of the first person, man or woman, to fly alone across the Atlantic nonstop from England to North America, from her childhood in Africa to her record-setting flight.
    ISBN 1-57505-081-1 (alk. paper)
    1. Markham, Beryl—Juvenile literature.  2. Women air pilots—Great Britain—Biography—Juvenile literature.  3. Women air pilots—Africa—Biography—Juvenile literature. [1. Markham, Beryl. 2. Air pilots. 3. Women—Biography.] I. Title.
II. Series.
TL540.M345B68   1998
629.13'092
[B]—DC21                                                                97-13649

Manufactured in the United States of America
1  2  3  4  5  6 – MA – 03  02  01  00  99  98

# Table of Contents

# 1

# When the Moon Shines at Midnight

Paddy wasn't an unusual sight for nine-year-old Beryl Clutterbuck, who had lived in British East Africa for as long as she could remember. She was used to seeing the neighbor's pet lion. But she hadn't expected to come upon him just in that place or quite at that moment. There he lay in a clearing near the neighbor's farmyard, "sprawled in the morning sun, huge . . . and gleaming with life," Beryl wrote. "His tail moved slowly, stroking the rough grass like a knotted rope end."

Beryl was a lot smaller than Paddy, but she was sure she had nothing to fear. After all, she knew all about lions. She looked straight at him and shuffled her bare feet in the dust. Then, to show Paddy she wasn't the least bit afraid, she started to sing an African marching song as she moved on past him, picking her way through the thick underbrush in search of adventure.

But Beryl should have paid closer attention to her father's warnings. Don't trust Paddy, he had told her many times. Lions are unpredictable. And sure enough, as soon as Beryl's back was turned, the lion pounced and sank his teeth into her leg. From somewhere deep down in his fur came a roar that seemed to fill the whole world. "I closed my eyes and tried not to be," Beryl wrote.

Beryl was rescued in time, and Paddy ran off. But before he was caught, he killed a horse, a cow, and a bull on a nearby farm.

Beryl was proud of the scars from Paddy's teeth and showed them off whenever she told this tale about growing up in Africa.

Beryl was born in England on October 26, 1902. When she was not quite two years old, her father, Charles Clutterbuck, left his family in England and went out to East Africa to seek his fortune.

At first, Charles worked as a dairy manager for another English settler, Lord Delamere. D, as he was called, lived with his wife near Njoro. Njoro was a small settlement just south of the equator, about a hundred miles northwest of the African frontier town of Nairobi. Njoro was in the highlands, perched on the edge of a gigantic split in the earth's surface known as the Great Rift Valley. In the ancient rock of its limestone cliffs were fossil remains of the first primates that had lived on the earth six million years before. The mornings at Njoro were sparkling and clear, the nights cool and fresh. Another English settler said, "Each day the light was different, and often the colors you saw yesterday never came back."

Charles wanted to start his own farm, and in 1905 he bought a thousand acres of untamed land near the Delameres. There was a citrus orchard on the property, and the farm came to be called Ndimu, which meant "lemon" in Swahili, the main language of East Africa. Much of the land was covered with thick grass and underbrush, known as bush. The growth was so dense that only huge knives like machetes could cut through. Behind this were forests of cedar, ebony, teak, olive, and bamboo. Some of the trees grew as high as two hundred feet, their branches brushing the sky.

Gradually Charles cleared enough land to plant fields of maize, a kind of corn. With power generated from two old train engines, he ground the yellow kernels into a coarse flour to feed the workers on the new Uganda Railway that passed across a corner of his land. The railway cut through the dense wilderness that stretched from the eastern coastal town of Mombasa all the way west to the shores of Lake Victoria on the Uganda border. People called it the "iron snake." The railroad was important to the settlers at Njoro because it brought things they badly needed—ploughs, barbed wire, beds, bathtubs, and bags of seed.

In addition to farming and milling, Charles trained thoroughbred horses. Racing was a favorite pastime among the European settlers. It wasn't long before Charles became known as the best racehorse trainer in East Africa.

Late in 1905, Clara Clutterbuck sailed from England with her three-year-old daughter, Beryl, and five-year-old son, Richard, to join Charles at Ndimu. Although many Europeans found the African wilderness beautiful and exciting and full of promise, Beryl's mother didn't like living there at all. She was used to the comfortable, safe surroundings of her home in England. Clara wasn't happy spending Christmas in a mud and thatch hut where cows stuck their heads through uncovered doors and windows. She didn't like sitting on chairs made of old packing crates and animal skins. And she was afraid of the lions and leopards who prowled around the farm at night, hunting the livestock.

Within a year of her arrival, Clara returned to England. Six-year-old Richard, whose health was poor, had been sent back with friends a few months earlier. Four-year-old Beryl stayed with her father at Ndimu.

In the coming months, Charles's farm prospered and grew. The small cluster of huts expanded into a settlement of wooden houses, barns, and stables. A thousand Africans lived and worked at Ndimu, looking after the livestock and tending the crops. A handful of them kept house for Beryl and her father—sweeping and scrubbing the floors and walls and cooking in big smoke-blackened iron pots on a wood stove.

Near the main house was Beryl's own hut. She shared it with Buller, a little black-and-white mutt who was a cross between a bull terrier and an English sheepdog. Lizards clung to the hut's mud walls with tiny claws. Invisible insects rustled in the tight latticework of the thatched roof. All around the hut hung charms that Beryl had made of bones and beads and tree bark to keep away evil spirits.

Beryl played with the animals on her father's farm. Besides a few stray lambs and goats, there were plenty of pigs, cows, horses, and chickens. Charles had two Great Danes, a couple of greyhounds named Storm and Sleet, and a parrot called Bombafu, which was Swahili for "fool."

Charles Clutterbuck was too busy to spend much time with his daughter, but Beryl didn't seem to mind. "People go around kissing and fussing over their children," she said when she was grown up. "I didn't get anything like that. I had to look after myself."

In fact, Beryl was loved and cared for by the Africans who worked on the farm. The Kikuyu, Kavirondo, and Nandi tribespeople treated her like one of their own *totos,* their boys.

Unlike other girls her age, Beryl was allowed to hunt and play with the young African boys. She spoke Swahili with them, went barefoot, and ate with her fingers. She wrestled with them, beat them at *bao* (a board game played with stones), and learned to jump higher than her head. She sat in their huts at night, listening to their grandmothers tell age-old stories of how people came to be on the earth. Beryl's friends called her Lakwana, which meant "little girl." They said she was very smart and had special *dawa,* or "magic powers."

Beryl's best friend was Kibii, a Nandi *toto*. His father, *arap* Maina, worked on the farm. *Arap* meant "son of" and was part of a man's name.

When Beryl wasn't playing with Kibii or Buller, she helped her father in the stables, grooming and pampering the beautiful, high-spirited horses. When she was six years old, he gave her a gentle chestnut pony named Wee MacGregor to ride.

Beryl was always happy in the stables, but life in the main house was quite another matter. Beryl's father had hired a governess named Emma Orchardson to live with them, hoping that she would be a motherly influence on his daughter. Emma's son Arthur came too. Beryl liked him and called him "little A." But she disliked and resented Emma, and she was confused about Emma's place in her home. Arthur always called her "Mummy," and pretty soon Beryl did too.

Emma Orchardson had her work cut out for her, trying to bring up a strong-willed tomboy who was used to taking orders only from her father, whom she adored. Beryl's determination to live life always on her own terms got in the way of Emma's plans.

Beryl used all her tricks to escape the influence of this woman. Sometimes she retreated to her own hut, or she slipped away to play with her African friends.

When Emma insisted that she come to the main house for lessons, Beryl ran off to the stables. She always chose a particularly unfriendly horse and hid in the back of its stall. Then, when Emma found Beryl and tried to coax her out, the horse would rear and bare its teeth and shake its hooves at the poor woman.

At other times, Beryl rode Wee MacGregor to Lord and Lady Delamere's farm. As her title suggested, Florence Delamere was very much a lady—graceful, charming, and beautiful. She was also courageous and hard-working and believed, like her husband, in the promising future of East Africa. The Delameres chose to live in a simple mud hut long after other settlers had built more permanent, comfortable houses. Sometimes when she visited, Beryl dressed up in the white frock that Lady D had given her and sat politely sipping tea among the fine Oriental rugs that were scattered on the dirt floor. Beryl thought of Lady D as her adopted mother. She liked Lord Delamere too. He was like an uncle to her, and she felt welcome in his house.

Beryl always got up early, before the gray sky had quite turned to morning and before her father woke up and reminded her to start the day with her grammar and arithmetic lessons. She popped out of bed, splashed her face with cold water from a stable bucket, and quickly dressed in her khaki shorts and shirt or her *lungi,* a length of cloth tied around her waist.

The smell and feel of the bush beckoned, dew and sunlight on the brown-gray of the dirt and the green-gray of the acacia trees. With her spear and her machete in hand and Buller trotting along beside her, Beryl would creep silently past the main house and run to join Kibii and the other *totos.* The village where they lived was only a short distance away, along an almost hidden path through the bush.

Outside a small cluster of log, mud, and thatch huts sat the old women of the village, their hands busy molding clay pots or weaving fiber bags to carry grain. The old men sat apart, talking among themselves. Cows, goats, sheep, and dogs snoozed in the shade or scratched in the dirt. A fence woven from the thorny branches of acacia trees circled the village to guard its inhabitants against predators.

One afternoon Beryl was hunting with Buller and *arap* Maina, Kibii's father. She had learned about the wild animals that lived in the bush and forest—their habits and hiding places, their speed and cunning. Like them, she could move through the underbrush without making a sound. Sometimes the hunting party brought a water buck or a gazelle home for dinner, or maybe a python or an ostrich. But on this particular day, they hoped to find a warthog, a kind of wild pig. Beryl knew that a warthog could be a deadly match for its enemy. Its wide, bristly snout was as strong as a battering ram, and the curved tusks of the male were deadly weapons.

Toward the end of the afternoon, Beryl, Buller, and *arap* Maina surprised a warthog peering out of its hole. It took off in a flash, and before anyone knew what was happening, Buller chased after it. The warthog was a good six times larger than the dog, but Buller was a brave hunter, and there was no calling him back.

Ignoring the nettles and thorns that scratched at her bare legs, Beryl ran in the direction of the scuffle. At first she followed the sound of Buller's barking. But soon she was tracking a trail of blood, which she feared was mostly Buller's.

When she found the two animals, the warthog was sitting under a thorn tree catching its breath. Buller lay on the ground nearby, his flesh torn clean away from his ribs. Without a second thought, Beryl aimed her spear at the pig's heart, pierced its tough, leathery hide, and killed it. Then she knelt down to let Buller lick her hand for comfort.

Beryl knew that the sun set quickly at the African equator. Almost without warning, daylight turned to dark, and the animals of the bush came out to feed. Soon lions and leopards would be prowling for their dinners. It wasn't a good idea to get in their way. By the time *arap* Maina caught up to Beryl, it was too dark to take Buller back to the farm. "When the moon shines at midnight," said *arap* Maina, "we will carry him home."

Buller lay unconscious in Beryl's lap while *arap* Maina told stories to help the time pass. When at last the moon lit their way back to the farm, Buller was barely alive. But Beryl nursed him day and night until he was better.

Survival, that was what mattered.

# 2

# A Horse with Wings

Beryl was a smart child. She read everything she could get her hands on, as long as it wasn't one of her schoolbooks. When she was thirteen, Charles and Emma decided it was time for her to follow an orderly plan of study and sent her off to boarding school. There, they thought, the company of well-mannered children and the discipline of the classroom might help to tame her. Beryl and Arthur went together to a school in Nairobi. Arthur liked it there and adjusted well. But for Beryl, the place was like a prison. She hated the confinement of solid walls and stupid rules. She didn't like the other students at the school. Except for Arthur, Beryl had never had any white friends, and she liked to think of herself as a *murani,* a young black warrior. Beryl made a point of misbehaving in one way or another, and after a few terms, she was expelled and sent home.

Beryl was very happy to be back at Ndimu, where her father had built her a new cedar shingle hut with three rooms, real glass windows, a wooden floor, and plenty of bookshelves. Unfortunately, Emma was still there. Lady D had died, so Beryl no longer had the only woman she trusted.

Beryl continued to help her father in the stables. She had a special way with horses and absolutely no fear. There wasn't a thoroughbred she couldn't ride. Sometimes she felt more at home on the back of a horse than on her own two feet.

Beryl spent a lot of time with Camsiscan, a three-year-old bay stallion with a black mane and a white star on his forehead. Every morning she brushed him down and cleaned his stall. Many nights she slept in the stable, curled up in the hay. Camsiscan watched Beryl silently, proud and aloof, unwilling to be tamed. One day, when she tried to ride him, he threw her. Another time he bit her hand as she brushed him. But the girl was as stubborn as the horse, and she gave him a sharp crack with the whip when he didn't follow her commands. After a while, Beryl and Camsiscan grew to understand and trust each other.

In 1916, the world war that had broken out in Europe two years earlier spread to East Africa, where Britain and its allies were trying to claim the African territories held by Germany. Most of the white settlers went to fight, as did many of the native Africans.

Among them was *arap* Maina, who was killed in the fighting in the neighboring country of Tanganyika. Beryl and Kibii didn't really understand what the war was all about. Once, when some soldiers from a British regiment stopped to rest at Ndimu, Charles explained, "They are fighting for your right to grow up." But that didn't make the loss of *arap* Maina any easier to accept.

One of the prize horses in the Clutterbuck stables was an Abyssinian mare named Coquette. Charles had bred her when Beryl was fourteen. Eleven months later, Coquette was ready to give birth. By this time, Beryl was quite experienced in foaling down thoroughbreds. She waited in Coquette's stall with two of her father's stable boys. No one expected anything to go wrong, but just in case, Beryl had her foaling kit ready, including a surgical knife and plenty of disinfectant.

Coquette lay on her side as Beryl and the two stable boys talked quietly, waiting. Finally, tiny hooves poked through the birth sac as the foal began to emerge. "Gently, gently, but strong and steady," Beryl later told the story, "I coax the new life into the glow of the stable lamp." She let Coquette rest a moment, then broke and removed the birth sac, tying and cutting the umbilical cord.

Beryl's father was watching from the door of the stable. "A fine job of work," he said to his daughter. "You brought him to life. He shall be yours."

The little colt was born at night, under the million stars of East Africa. Beryl remembered a story from Greek mythology that Charles used to tell her. It was about a horse called Pegasus who had wings and flew across the sky. There was a constellation of stars named after the horse with wings. Beryl decided to call her new colt Pegasus.

Beryl was beginning to grow into a young woman. When she was only sixteen, she became engaged to a man from one of the neighboring farms. His name was Jock Purves. He was in his early thirties, a former Scottish rugby player who had recently returned from the war. Jock was a likable man—smart, kind, strong, and athletic. According to rumors in Njoro, Beryl's father owed him money, and Jock was willing to forget the debt if Beryl agreed to marry him. Beryl agreed. The wedding was in Nairobi on October 15, 1919, just before Beryl's seventeenth birthday. After a honeymoon in India, they returned to live on Jock's farm.

The year after Beryl and Jock were married, a severe drought hit East Africa. The equatorial sun parched the land for weeks. The bush and forest lost their earthy smells, and soft greens turned to a lifeless brown. Both wild animals and livestock began to die of thirst. Vultures circled overhead, watching and waiting.

Without his crops, Charles couldn't keep the farm going. Ndimu was sold, and the house and most of the horses were auctioned off. As the train carried away the last of Charles Clutterbuck's possessions, Beryl said, "It carried with it most of my youth—my father's title to the farm, the buildings, the stables, and all of the horses, except just one—the one with wings."

# 3

# Engines Are Moody Things

In the face of bankruptcy, Charles took a job as a racehorse trainer in Peru, almost halfway around the world. After her father left Africa, Beryl worked with the thoroughbreds in Jock's stables. It wasn't long before the horses she trained began to win races, and her reputation spread quickly. When she was only eighteen, she became the first woman in Kenya to get a horse trainer's license.

But Beryl and Jock weren't getting along very well. She told some of her friends that Jock was boring, others that he drank too much, but it wasn't clear what was happening. Her thin, oval face rarely showed what she was really thinking, but chances are, she was simply too independent to be happy with Jock.

Sometimes she left Jock and went to stay with her friends Karen Blixen and Denys Finch Hatton at the Blixen farm near Nairobi. Karen was a Danish writer whom Beryl had known since childhood, and they often went riding together. Denys was tall and good-looking, "a great hunter and a great, a tremendous personality," said Beryl. He taught Beryl to love good books and good music and to believe in herself. She looked up to Denys as she had looked up to her father.

In 1924, Beryl finally left Jock Purves for good. Riding Pegasus, she followed the trail to Molo, a small settlement just half a day's ride to the north. She knew good trainers there who could help her start her own business.

Beryl brought only two saddlebags to Molo with her. For Pegasus, she had packed a currycomb, a sack of crushed oats, a blacksmith's knife, and a horse thermometer. "For me the bags held pajamas, slacks, a shirt, toothbrush, and comb," she remembered. "I never owned less, nor can I be sure that I ever needed more."

Everything else was gone. Even the name of Beryl's country had changed after the war, from British East Africa to Kenya Colony. "All these were behind me," she said, "not like part of a life, but like a whole life lived and ended." Buller too was buried back at Ndimu.

Beryl didn't like Molo very much. It was cold and bleak, and she missed the dry, sunny days at Njoro. Back at the farm, Beryl had been her father's helper, watching and learning while he was in charge. At Molo, she was a head trainer, with no one else to share responsibility or make decisions. A few of Charles's stable boys had followed her on foot from Ndimu to groom the horses and clean the stalls. But, Beryl realized, "They cannot apply a pressure bandage, or treat lameness, or judge fitness, or handle an over-willing horse. . . . These things belong to me." She worked in the stables from dawn to dusk, but the days were never long enough to do all that had to be done.

One night, Beryl heard a voice outside the door of her hut. *"Hodi,"* it said, "I am here." It was too dark outside to see anyone, but she sensed that the visitor was friendly. *"Kaaribu,"* she said. "Come, you are welcome." A tall, solemn man stepped into the hut. A lion's claw hung at his chest. Around his waist was a beaded belt, and on his ankles he wore bracelets made from the tails of black-and-white colobus monkeys. "I am *arap* Ruta," he said to Beryl. "I have come to help—to work for you, if you can use me."

It was her childhood friend Kibii. He had left Njoro a boy and returned a grown man, a *murani* or warrior. When he found that Beryl was no longer at Ndimu, he had followed her to Molo. Beryl knew that she and *arap* Ruta would become friends again. But their friendship would have restrictions they had not known as children. To the rest of the world, Beryl was a European woman with white skin. *Arap* Ruta was a man, a black African. She was now his boss, and he her servant.

Although Beryl was as strong as a man and more capable than most, she needed *arap* Ruta's help with her greatest weakness—dealing with people. They worked well together. Before long, with ten horses to train, they outgrew the stables at Molo and moved to better quarters in the nearby town of Nakuru. Beryl's reputation spread, and she became known as Memsahib wa Farasi, "Lady of the Horses."

One day she was riding Pegasus along a dusty road. She came upon a man standing beside a stalled automobile. He was tinkering with something under the hood, trying to urge the stubborn machine back to life. Beryl had no patience with these new inventions.

They were always running out of fuel or conking out for some reason or other.

She stopped to chat with the stranger. He liked driving motor cars in spite of their moody engines, he told her. After all, he said, you have to worry about something. "You couldn't just sit on this window ledge of Africa and watch the clouds go by." To Beryl, the automobile was an unwelcome visitor. It didn't belong here. But she'd have to get used to it, the man said, because cars were definitely coming. And, he added, so were the "interesting inventions" the British called aeroplanes.

The man's name was Tom Campbell Black. He had good reason to know about aeroplanes because he flew one. Beryl found him interesting, but she didn't really take this flying business seriously. People weren't birds. Why should they try to sprout wings!

Tom started his automobile and drove off. Beryl rode Pegasus back to the stables. But over the next few weeks, her thoughts kept going back to something Tom had said. "When you fly, you get a feeling of possession that you couldn't have if you owned all of Africa," he told her. "You feel that everything you see belongs to you—all the pieces are put together, and the whole is yours. . . . It makes you feel bigger than you are." Although Beryl didn't like the idea of aeroplanes buzzing overhead, Tom's words stayed with her.

The horses that Beryl was training began to win important races. She became the first woman, and the youngest person, to be well respected in Kenyan racing circles. She would not have had such recognition in England, where women weren't taken seriously as trainers for many years. But in a country like Kenya, there were opportunities for any man or woman with the determination and skill to snatch them up. For Beryl, a race was the sum of all the things that horse and trainer and jockey put into it. "Skill and reason and chance run with them," she used to explain. "Courage runs with them—and strategy."

When Beryl was twenty-three, she decided to enter Wise Child, one of the best thoroughbreds in her stable, in the big Saint Leger race. The horse's legs were not very strong, but Beryl had twelve weeks to work with her. If anyone could turn Wise Child into a competitive racer, it was the Lady of the Horses.

Finally the day of the great race came. Now and then a nervous murmur stirred the crowd. Otherwise all was quiet in the stands. Every eye was on the starting gates, and it seemed as if no one were breathing. Then the gates snapped open, and the crowd shouted, "They're off!"

In the lead, only a few yards from the finish line, one of Wise Child's legs gave out. But as a thousand people watched, she crossed the finish line on three legs, winning the Saint Leger race and breaking the course speed record.

Despite her success, Beryl was restless, always dreaming of new adventures and new worlds to conquer. A year after Wise Child's victory, Beryl became engaged to Mansfield Markham, the wealthy son of an English baronet. Mansfield had come to Kenya to explore and hunt. He was tall, thin, fair-haired, good-looking, intelligent, and quiet. Beryl wasn't in love with him, but she liked him well enough. And with her father so far away, she looked for another man to depend on. Beryl and Mansfield were married on September 3, 1927, in Nairobi. Lord Delamere gave her away.

A little over a year after their marriage, Beryl sailed to England to give birth to a son, Gervase. A few months later, she and Mansfield separated. Beryl didn't want a child, and she left Gervase in England with Mansfield's mother.

When Beryl Markham returned to Kenya in 1930, she was twenty-eight years old. Charles Clutterbuck had come home from Peru, and Beryl spent the next few months working in her father's stables.

Beryl's old friend Denys Finch Hatton was learning to fly, and he took her up a few times in his two-seater biplane—a de Havilland Gipsy Moth. She loved the feel of the wind and the adventure of flying.

One night, several months later, Beryl was in Nairobi with friends. As they stood in a field on the edge of town, talking and watching the stars, they heard a humming sound from somewhere in the darkness. When the noise came closer, they saw the intruder, a monoplane circling overhead. Beryl and her friends lit flares and turned on the headlights of their two motor cars to guide the plane in for a landing. The pilot stepped out of the cockpit, dusty and unshaven. It was Tom Black.

Beryl and Tom sat at an all-night café, drinking coffee and talking about Tom's adventures. He had recently logged six thousand air miles, flying from London to Nairobi and then into the bush to rescue a wounded hunter. Many people thought that although planes had proven useful in World War I, they didn't have much potential for peacetime. But Tom knew better. He had no doubt that aviation was going to be very important in the future. Kenya didn't have many roads, and Tom's plan was to deliver mail around the country by aeroplane. Daylight came, and as Tom went off in search of sleep, he said to Beryl, "Of course you're going to fly. I've always known it. I could see it in the stars."

Soon after meeting with Tom, Beryl told *arap* Ruta that she had decided to give up horses for aeroplanes. *Arap* Ruta was suspicious of fast-moving machines, but loyalty came before caution. "If it is to be that we must fly, Memsahib, then we will fly," he said. "At what hour of the morning do we begin?" Keeping only Pegasus, Beryl turned her stable of horses over to other trainers and moved with *arap* Ruta to Nairobi.

In April 1931, Tom began teaching Beryl to fly. She sat behind him in the cockpit of a Gipsy Moth and learned about ailerons, rudders, and flaps—parts of the plane that help the pilot steer. He showed her how they worked in takeoffs, landings, and down-drafts, and how they affected turning, banking, and climbing. She learned how to use the joystick, a lever that juts straight up from the floor of the cockpit, to steer the plane and adjust its altitude. Tom was a good instructor—careful, thorough, and patient. He let Beryl make her own mistakes and figure out how to correct them.

In May, Denys invited Beryl to fly to the coast with him. But Tom had a bad feeling about the trip. He reminded Beryl that she had scheduled a lesson with him that day, so she decided not to go. On Denys's return to Nairobi, his plane burst into flames and crashed.

Beryl took Denys's death very hard, but it was a turning point for her. A month after he died, she took up flying lessons again, determined to become one of the best pilots in East Africa.

# 4

# The Rest Is Up to You

Beryl's first solo flight was on June 11, 1931. It was expected to last about five minutes. She was to take off, climb to eight hundred feet, circle the field, and land. In 1931 in Kenya, this was not so easy. The runway was a dirt track, full of warthog holes and anthills and wild animals wandering out of the bush in search of water.

The takeoff went well, and Beryl cruised through the air at eighty miles per hour, singing to herself. So far so good. Next she had to make a perfect three-point landing, with the two wheels touching down at exactly the same moment as the tail skid. And she must maintain just the right speed. If she was going too fast, the plane would bump and bounce on the ground. If she came in too slowly, she would make a pancake landing, plopping down flat with a thud. Tom watched proudly as Beryl completed her flight without mishap.

Tom taught Beryl that there were two things she must learn to trust. One was her compass. "It will tell you where you ought to be going." The other was her instincts. "And the rest is up to you," he said. Beryl also relied on her chief mechanic, *arap* Ruta, who made sure that everything was in perfect working order. He groomed the plane as if it were a prize horse, touching it with care and respect, and speaking to it with soft words.

Over the next two years, Beryl added miles and experience to her flying record. She needed a total of one thousand hours of solo flight for her commercial pilot's license.

She had to pass written tests on aviation law and air navigation. And she must show that she could strip a plane's engine, clean the jets and filters, change the spark plugs, and adjust the points. In addition to understanding everything about an aeroplane, Beryl said, "I learned what every dreaming child needs to know—that no horizon is so far that you cannot get above it or beyond it."

In September 1933, Beryl got her commercial pilot's license, allowing her to carry paying passengers. She was the first woman in Kenya—and one of the first women in the world—to do so.

Charles Clutterbuck was proud of Beryl, but he refused to fly with her. Aeroplanes had no appeal for him. Why were people in such a hurry to get places? "Fly if you like," he told his daughter, "but don't ask me to go up there."

A few commercial air services had started up in East Africa. They were hiring pilots to fly passengers and supplies from place to place. Soon Beryl was earning her living as a pilot for East African Airways. She carried mail and food to gold miners in the neighboring country of Tanganyika. If a hunter was sick or injured in the bush, she delivered medical supplies or flew him to the hospital in Nairobi.

After a few months with East African Airways, Beryl worked as a private pilot, carrying passengers wherever they wanted to go. By the time she was thirty, she had saved enough money to buy her own plane, a silver and blue Avro Avian.

When she was flying, Beryl was far more afraid of doing something wrong than of mechanical failure, bad weather, or any other danger. She had learned from the *toto*s at Njoro that mistakes bring shame and humiliation. In Beryl's mind, nothing could be worse. But she needn't have worried. She was an excellent pilot. "Her navigation was uncanny," a colleague said. "She could find her way to any spot. . . . I never saw her make a poor landing, even in really filthy weather."

When Beryl was thirty-one, she decided to try something more exciting and profitable. Denys Finch Hatton had once told her that white hunters might be interested in hiring private pilots to fly over the bush and spot elephants for them. Then the hunters would track the animals on foot and kill them for their valuable ivory tusks. Without the help of an aeroplane, a hunting party could spend weeks slashing a trail through the bush in search of a good herd.

From the distance of a plane, an elephant looks about as big as a mouse and is well camouflaged. But Beryl soon learned to spot the animals, judge the size of their tusks, and determine the herd's exact location. Then, with her compass, a good sense of direction, and sharp eyes, she always found her way back to the hunters' camp to make her report.

Tom Black had taken a pilot's job in England. He sent Beryl a letter begging her to give up elephant scouting. It was too dangerous, he said, "sheer madness." There were always disasters waiting to happen in the bush—sudden storms and malaria and tsetse fly bites. Every pilot feared the razor-sharp sansevieria plant, which skewered any plane that tried to land on it. And worst of all were the siafu ants who swarmed over a live animal or person and cleaned the flesh from its bones within a matter of hours.

Beryl thought a lot about Tom's warning letter. Just as often, she asked herself, "What if I should fly away one morning and not come back?" But the answer to her own question was always, "If the engine fails me, if a quick storm drives me into the bush . . . well, that is the chance and that is the job."

# 5

# The Earth in the Palm of Your Hand

When she was thirty-three years old, Beryl decided to say *kwaheri,* "good-bye," to Kenya for a while and follow Tom Black to England. She sold her Avian and bought a new Leopard Moth. She said good-bye to her father, who was moving to South Africa, and to her oldest and most loyal friend, *arap* Ruta. Then she took off from Nairobi and flew across North Africa, the Mediterranean Sea, and the English Channel with only a few maps and a compass to guide her. By this time, Beryl figured, she had logged a total of two thousand hours in the air and a quarter of a million flight miles.

For several months, Beryl worked as chief pilot for Air Cruisers Limited. She also visited her six-year-old son, Gervase, who still lived with his grandmother. One day she ran into an old acquaintance from Kenya, a man named John Carberry. Carberry was disagreeable and gruff, but he had money and influence, and Beryl knew he could be useful to her. One evening, at a dinner party, he made her an offer. If Beryl agreed to fly alone, nonstop, from England to New York, he would let her use his own plane. No pilot, man or woman, had ever flown solo from England to America without stopping along the way.

Prevailing head winds made the east-west flight across the Atlantic especially difficult. Three pilots—Jim Mollison, John Grierson, and Amy Johnson—had completed the east-west water jump, as pilots liked to call it. But Grierson had made stops along the way, and Mollison had flown solo from Ireland to Canada and later with Johnson from Wales. Other pilots had tried and failed. Some gave up because of bad weather. Others crashed. A few simply disappeared.

Beryl hoped to set off across the Atlantic Ocean in August 1936, but it was hard to set a definite date. Carberry's plane, a Vega Gull designed by Edgar Percival, still had to be completed and tested. But if the flight was delayed too long, the unpredictable weather conditions of late autumn would make the journey impossible.

During the long weeks of waiting, Tom Black kept Beryl busy. She spent hours swimming, running, jumping rope, and riding horses in training for the exhausting flight. She and Tom studied the maps and flight logs of earlier transatlantic pilots, making note of their successes and mistakes. Tom introduced Beryl to Jim Mollison, who added his own stories. And Beryl made frequent visits to Percival's factory to talk to the engineers and watch the plane take shape.

The plane was christened *The Messenger.* Its body was made of wood and painted turquoise blue with silver wings. The cockpit was just big enough for two seats and two fuel tanks. Additional tanks were located in the wings and in the center section of the main body, giving the plane a total fuel capacity of 255 gallons. With a two-hundred horsepower engine and an electrically operated propeller, the Vega Gull was expected to fly for 3,800 miles before needing to refuel. The flight would be 3,600 miles long.

By the middle of August 1936, *The Messenger* was ready. Time was running short, and Beryl made only two quick trial flights. Edgar Percival gave her a few final instructions. She must remember to let the engine stall on empty before opening up a reserve fuel tank. Otherwise, he warned, the engine would airlock, and the fuel wouldn't flow evenly. But if she followed his directions exactly, he promised, the engine would start again. Beryl was nervous about the flight, but long ago she had learned to make fear work for her.

On September 4, Beryl decided to take off. *The Messenger* was at the Royal Air Force base at Abingdon, fifty miles from London. The plane was heavy with fuel and would need every inch of the mile-long runway to gather enough speed for takeoff. Even then no one could be sure that the Vega Gull would get off the ground. But pilot and plane were ready. The winds were strong and gusty, and officers at the air force base thought Beryl was crazy to attempt the flight under such conditions. But according to weather reports, it was as good as she could hope for at this time of year.

Tom Black hadn't thought she would take off that day, given the weather, so he wasn't there to see her off. But he had told her earlier, "I'm glad you're going to do it . . . . It won't be simple . . . . The wind's against you . . . . So is the weather. You won't have a radio. If you misjudge your course only a few degrees, you'll end up in Labrador or in the sea."

Dressed in her white flying suit, Beryl climbed into the cockpit. She had with her a thermos of coffee, a flask of brandy, a bag of nuts and dried fruit, a few pieces of cold chicken, her maps and compass, and her log book. She wore Jim Mollison's watch for good luck. It had crossed the Atlantic twice. "Don't get it wet," he told her. The fuel tanks in the cabin took up so much room that she decided to leave her bulky life jacket behind. As she buckled her helmet, Beryl called from the plane, *"Twende tu,"* Swahili for "I'm going."

It was just before 7:00 P.M. when she took off. As Jim Mollison watched her go, he said, "That's the last we'll see of Beryl." Six hundred yards down the runway, she was airborne. Perhaps the Vega Gull would be spotted by a ship that happened to sail beneath her flight path. Otherwise, *The Messenger* and its pilot would not be heard from again until they landed—if they landed.

About half an hour after she took off from Abingdon, Beryl flew over the coast of Ireland. It was the last land she was to see for many hours. It was raining in the darkness around her, and the wind blew hard. There were no instruments to show her exactly where she was or how far she had yet to go. Beryl was totally isolated from the rest of the world. But she felt confident. Jim Mollison's watch told her how long she had been flying, and the altimeter told her that she was at two thousand feet above sea level.

Although her map was only a piece of paper with some lines on it, Beryl imagined it was saying, "Read me carefully, follow me closely. . . . I am the earth in the palm of your hand."

Several hours into the flight, the Vega Gull's engine coughed a few times and died. The steady drone of the plane gave way to the silence of the night. Beryl's strongest impulse was to pull back on the joystick. But she knew she must do just the opposite and push the stick forward, even though doing so would cause the plane to nose downward toward the water. The altimeter already showed that she was losing altitude. Her hands, if not her mind, started to follow Edgar Percival's orders. In the dark, she found her flashlight and shone it on the reserve tank. She opened the valve and waited for the fuel to feed and restart the engine. After about thirty seconds, the engine spluttered to life, just as Percival had promised. Beryl pulled back the joystick and regained altitude. *The Messenger* had dived to only three hundred feet above the water.

Darkness fell, and Beryl flew blind for almost twenty hours. The weather was terrible. "I couldn't see anything beyond my wingtips," she wrote. "If I climbed it was sleet, if I dropped it was rain. If I skimmed the sea it was fog."

The plane pitched and tossed in the wind. Beryl became disoriented. Once, when lightning flashed, she looked out the window of the plane and saw the sky below and the sea above. She was flying upside down.

Beryl later wrote: "Being alone in an aeroplane for even so short a time as a night and a day... with nothing to observe but your instruments and your own hands in semi-darkness, nothing to contemplate but the size of your small courage, nothing to wonder about but the beliefs, the faces, and the hopes rooted in your mind—such an experience can be as startling as the first awareness of a stranger walking by your side at night. You are the stranger."

To keep her mind off the endless darkness, Beryl thought of her home and her friends in Africa. At dawn there was a break in the fog, and she saw the coast of Newfoundland. "I've never seen land so beautiful," she wrote.

By this time, *The Messenger* was on its last fuel tank. The gauge showed it was almost empty, and so Beryl decided to make a refueling stop at Sydney Airport in Nova Scotia before flying the last few hours to New York.

Just then, the engine began to splutter. Beryl looked for someplace to land. "I saw that I had to come down and made for the beach. I couldn't land there; there was nothing but great big rocks and *Messenger* and I would have been dashed to pieces. I went inland." And then the engine stopped.

Beryl managed to bring the plane down into what she thought was a field. But within a few seconds, the left wheel caught in a patch of mud, and the plane did a nosedive. Beryl's head hit the windshield, and she passed out.

She had landed in a rocky peat bog, twelve miles short of the Sydney Airport. It was twenty-one hours and twenty-five minutes since she had taken off, and forty hours since she had last slept.

When Beryl came to, she climbed out of the cockpit and started to wade through the bog for help. Half an hour later, waist-deep in mud, blood running from her forehead, she was found by two fishermen who took her to a nearby farmhouse, made her a cup of tea, and sent her off in a taxi to the nearest hospital.

John Carberry was waiting in New York for Beryl's arrival. She telephoned him from Newfoundland to report that *The Messenger* was in pretty bad shape. The engine was torn off, the propeller smashed, and the landing gear completely gone. "Leave it there," he told her. "Don't worry about it."

It was only an aeroplane, after all. The most important thing was that Beryl herself had survived.

# Afterword

Beryl's transatlantic flight brought her world fame at the age of thirty-four. The press went crazy over this amazing woman, and people everywhere praised her courage and skill. Beryl loved all the attention, even though she always remained modest about her accomplishments.

During the next several years, Beryl lived in New York, California, New Mexico, and London, mingling with famous people and spending more money than she had. She married again—an American writer named Raoul Schumacher. She wrote *West with the Night*, a book about her life in Africa and her transatlantic flight, in addition to several short stories.

By the late 1940s, Beryl was once again restless and unhappy. She had given up writing and flying and had no idea what to do next. She had proven that she could ride any horse anywhere and fly a plane under impossible conditions, but she had trouble coping with daily matters. After a while, Beryl decided to return home to Africa.

With the help of friends, she started up her horse training business again, this time at Naro Moru, a small settlement in the grasslands at the base of Mount Kenya. An Irish jockey named Buster Parnell joined her, and together, as trainer and rider, they were unbeatable. Beryl's horses won race after race.

Beryl could be difficult and ornery, but even people who didn't like her respected her. When she walked into a room, she looked like a golden lioness. With her talent and glamour, she became a legend.

Although Beryl hadn't flown for many years, her name was listed among the great long-distance aviators of that time—Charles Lindbergh, Amelia Earhart, Wiley Post, and Amy Johnson. England's Royal Air Force planned a celebration for the fiftieth anniversary of *The Messenger's* transatlantic flight. Beryl hoped to go to London for the occasion, but six weeks before the event, she tripped over her dog and broke her hip. Shortly after surgery, she developed pneumonia. She died a few weeks later, on August 3, 1986, at the age of eighty-three.

The anniversary celebration was marked by a service at Saint Clement Dane's Church in London. It was also a celebration of Beryl's life. A friend stood before a full congregation of writers, aviators, racers—British, American, and Kenyan—to pay tribute. "Around Beryl life was never dull," he said. "Like a comet passing through the firmament she lit up all around her. . . . *Kwaheri,* Beryl; God bless you and God speed."

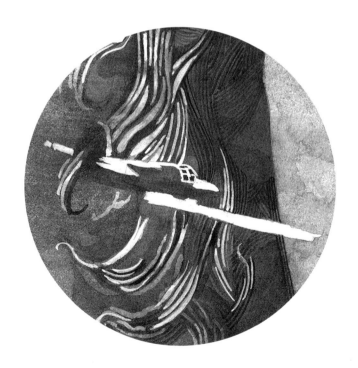

# Bibliography

Allen, John E. *Early Aircraft.* New York: Macmillan, 1976.

Boyne, Walter J. *The Smithsonian Book of Flight for Young People.* New York: Atheneum, 1988.

Dinesen, Isak. *Out of Africa.* New York: Vintage Books, 1965.

——. *Shadows on the Grass.* New York: Vintage Books, 1974.

Huxley, Elspeth. *The Flame Trees of Thika.* New York: Penguin Books, 1982.

——. *The Mottled Lizard.* New York: Penguin Books, 1982.

Lovell, Mary S. *Straight on Till Morning: The Biography of Beryl Markham.* New York: St. Martin's Press, 1987.

Markham, Beryl. *The Splendid Outcast: Beryl Markham's African Stories.* San Francisco: North Point Press, 1987.

——. *West with the Night.* San Francisco: North Point Press, 1983.

Rosenblum, Richard. *Wings: The Early Years of Aviation.* New York: Four Winds Press, 1980.

Trzebinski, Errol. *The Lives of Beryl Markham.* New York: W. W. Norton, 1993.

*World without Walls: Beryl Markham's African Memoir.* San Francisco: KQED, 1985. Documentary.

# Index

# About the Author

**Andy Russell Bowen** has been on seven photographic safaris in east, central, and southern Africa. She enjoys travel in many other parts of the world as well. With a master's degree in English, she has taught creative writing in elementary grades and has written several children's plays. Andy lives in Minneapolis with her husband and has a grown daughter in Santa Fe. This is her fourth Creative Minds book.

# About the Illustrator

**Shelly O. Haas** sees Beryl Markham, child of Africa, as a free spirit. Beryl rose to the occasion throughout her life because she knew that she could. As the daughter of a British pioneer in and out of the local tribal village, she was able to set her own standards without the boundaries of culture or gender that limited other women of her time. As an adult, she was most at home alone in the sky. Shelly hopes her images best reflect Beryl as an individual in a life without context. Shelly has illustrated fourteen books for children and enjoys her life as an illustrator and mother in Harrington, Washington.